A Pandemic Response
~ in Poetic Verse ~

By Patrice Lee

A Pandemic Response by Patrice Lee
Copyright 2022

Printed in the United States of America
Publisher: Feinstein Development and Associates, LLC
d/b/a Leep4Joy Books

All rights reserved. No part of the book may be reproduced, copied, or transmitted in any form, or by any means without written consent from the author.

Identifiers: ISBN # 978-1-7326210-4-6

Edited by: P. A. Fort
Cover Design: Francesco Paolo Ardizzone
Page layout: Patrice Lee

Please send all correspondence to:
Feinstein Development and Associates, P.O. Box 48172 Oak Park, MI 48237 or via Email to:
PatriceALee@gmail.com

Table of Contents

"Circumstances" Happen 7

A "Circumstance" Called Corona 15

School Matters. 21

Dear God! (Smile!) 27

Choose Kindness. 41

Pandemic Response—An Adult Perspective 45

A Reflection of Yesterday 51

Pandemic News 55

Gratitude and Sorrow 67

It's a Different World Now 77

Race, Creed, and Color 83

Healing is a Process 89

A Real Friend. 97

Little Life Lessons to Live By 105

~

Introduction

When faced with adversity, we respond. When a deadly pandemic grips the world, a nation, and its' people adjust and adapt to a new way of living life. Pandemic 2020 has turned our lives upside down.

Consequently, children have questions. They need answers, and want to know what happened, and why? ...Where it came from? ...What we're going to do about it? {And} ...When it will be over?

How do you respond to these questions when no one has real, definitive answers? Though probable solutions change from day to day, we must help children have hope for a brighter future.

On the pages that follow, the poems are meant to describe what children, and adults alike, are experiencing, as well as, provide encouragement. Even if things don't return to normal right away; children need to know that "coronavirus" is just one of the many "circumstances" of life.

May "A Pandemic Response" be a "gentle" reminder of how far we've come since the beginning of Pandemic 2020. And may it offer hope to those who read it in the years ahead. As you reflect on the recent events, and your personal journey through it, "rejoice" for you are yet alive!

May the peace that surpasses all understanding keep, and sustain you, until this season we're in is over. Presenting conversational poetry children and adults can relate to.

"Circumstances" Happen

Children's thoughts are innocent and pure, honest, thought-provoking, and sincere. Children usually say what comes to mind, dispersing words not given to time or season, pouring out from the heart with, or without, rhyme or reason.

Children need to know that "circumstances" can-and-will happen, and are a natural part of living {life}; and to understand that every "circumstance" is subject to change. Even if we can't promise change right away, a child can be comforted by our positive stance.

Sometimes they just need to be comforted or consoled, and to know most trouble doesn't last forever—that it's not here to stay. Like adults, they just want to know that it's going to be okay.

"*When I was a child, I spake as a child, I understood as a child, I thought as a child...*" (1 Corinthians 13:11).

"Circumstances" Happen to Everyone
{A conversation between two children}

I have a "circumstance." Do you?

Yes, I have one too. But, Mom says,
"Circumstances" happen to everyone.
Though they teach us lessons,
They're never fun.

Well, another "circumstance" has just begun.

Oh-oh! There's another "circumstance" to overcome? But we just got over the other one!

It'll be okay, 'cause "circumstances"
Don't usually last that long.

Well, we can still have fun!
Wanna' play tag?

Okay. You're it!

12.20.20

I've Got a **"Circumstance!"**
{a preteen growing up}

I've got a "circumstance,"
But, I'm gonna be just fine.

It's just another "circumstance"
I'm going through; for
"Circumstances" come and go.
They are nothing new.

As long as I keep a joyful heart,
and peace of mind,
I know I'll be just fine.

"Circumstance!"

"Circumstance!"
Today it's this thing!
Tomorrow it's that!

What you must remember, and
Come to understand is, no matter
How great the "circumstances" you must face,
They are no greater than you can stand.

In each and every "circumstance,"
Your attitude about it can
Determine the outcome in the end.

The sooner you adjust it upward,
The sooner you can look back on where
You've been.

01.27.17

My "Circumstance"

My "circumstance" may not be
Your "circumstance." But,
In each one there's a lesson to learn;
And we react to our "circumstances" differently.
Some of us sing, and some of us cry;
…Can't always tell you "how" or "why."

Perhaps this "circumstance" happened to you; or
Maybe it happened to someone at school.
Not long ago it happened to me! No matter
How remarkably different we might be,
I know you'll come through your
"circumstance" too,
…and do it successfully!

12.20.20

Hope in the Middle of "Circumstance"

Life is full of "circumstances"
But as we learn to cope,
Right-in-the-middle-of each "circumstance,"
We'll always find **hope**.

So keep lookin' up my friend,
As things will surely turn around.
For even the darkest moment,
Can end on a positive note.

{Revised 01.03.22}

A "Circumstance" called *Corona*

A "pandemic" is a form of adversity, which poses challenges for all mankind to overcome. I refer to it as a "circumstance"-- one of many "circumstances" of life. Unlike most "circumstances," this one has a name. They call it "coronavirus."

This "Circumstance!"
{"Corona"}

'When a "circumstance" happens it's usually
Something we can't control, for "circumstances"
Happen to all of us, young, and old.
Sometimes we get over them really fast.
Then, there are the kind that last and last.
~
This one came when I was only six.
Now I'm seven, and it still hasn't been fixed.
I hope it'll be over by the time I'm eight,
'Cuz I want to be back to normal by a certain date.

It's going to be my birthday again!
Nothing's the same since this "circumstance" began.
I miss my friends, and family too.
I want to hear them sing,
"Happy Bi-r-r-r-thday to You!"
"Happy Bi-r-r-r-thday to You!"
{sing it}
~
"Be patient," Mom said. It's happened to everyone.
But, I can't help it! ! ! I miss having fun!
Well, I guess I'll go back to my computer--school,
'Cuz the teacher's waiting. The class is too.

12.20.20

It's "*Corona*" -- Stay Home
{from the *heart* of a child}

A "circumstance" has come my way.
School was cancelled again--yesterday.
The principal said, "Our safety comes first."
But, does he know how much it hurts?

It's called "corona," and it's quite unique.
Things don't look good. They called it "bleak."
What do you mean, "…things don't look good?"
It might help some, if I understood!

'Cuz everything looks the same to me.
I wake up. I get dressed. I brush my teeth.
It's just we've stayed home again--unexpectedly.
And now I'm home all the time, with family.

~

Well, things are changing for all of us.
We walk to the park now. We don't take the bus.
We spend more time together.
And sometimes we fuss. But, more importantly,
We've learned to value being kind to one another,
And how to do things more lovingly.

03.03.21

~

A "Circumstance" called Corona!

Child: Mom, why did corona have to come?
Mom: My child, you've asked a question
   that puzzles everyone.

Child: Well, when do you think it's gonna leave?
Mom: No one knows for sure, but we hope—soon.

Child: What can we do about it today?
Mom: Well honey, we can always pray,
   …'Cuz prayer changes things.

04. 08.21

No Ordinary "Circumstance"
{A brief conversation between two adults}

It's just another "circumstance."

No. It's not the same!

This is no ordinary "circumstance."
This one is different.
The others didn't bother me like this one.

Well, I sure hope it leaves here just
as quickly as it came.

03.03.21

School Matters

School Daze--@ Home

We begin early in the morning
And work 'til late at night.
We've rearranged all the furniture to be just right.
But since we've settled in at home for school
We have less free time, ...more work to do.

I miss playing with friends old and new,
I miss snacks and recess too.
It seems like our day never ends.
Will we ever go back to school?
I wonder if, and when?

I'm Ready to Go to School

They say we've got a "circumstance"
We've got to get through; and
Everyone's been inconvenienced,
Including me-and-you. Oh how
I miss my friends and classmates.
I miss the teachers too.

I'm ready to get back to normal, and
I want to go to school.
I promise to study this time, and
I'll obey all the rules.
Will you open the building please?
...Because I'm ready to go to school.

03.03.21

Screen Time
(Every ten minutes the screen blinks.)

I stare at the computer because
It's been really hard for me to think.
...Can't remember what I learned yesterday;
...Feels like a missing link.

When the teacher ask a question,
My confidence begins to shrink. For
Each time I have the right answer,
My screen starts to blink.

Though the class is ahead of me,
I'm trying to catch up.
I'll be glad when the virus is over,
'Cuz I've really had enough.

Dear Principal _____,

My Mom is...,
I think the word is "agitated."
The virus is getting on her nerves
And I don't know what to do.
Is your office open? May I come talk to you?
Do I need to make an appointment before I get to school?

And if the doors aren't open, what should I do?
...'Cuz I really need to talk to you.
Mom always says, "I'm too noisy," and that
I need to "be quiet when I walk."

Will your door be open?
Ple-e-e-e-ase, can we talk?

By the way, I'm gonna be a better person.
I think school's a pretty awesome place.
Just hope it won't be much longer, 'cuz
Mom said, "We're runnin' out of space."

03.03.21

{Not sure what Mom means, because we have the same space we've always had? ? ?}

"May I Come In?"
{student}

I went to school today because
They said it would be open,
But it was closed again.
I'm tired of being at home.
"May I please come in?"

I've been at home studying. This is day ten.
I don't need to understand "how-or-why."
I just want to know when
I can go back to school again?

And when I get there tomorrow,
"May I ple-e-e-ease come in?"

{Now} If this is an extended vacation,
I'm ready for it to end.
'Cuz I really do miss school, and
I really miss my friends.
The next time I come to school,
Please open the door and let me in.

03.03.21

"Dear God, ...I Need to Talk to You"

If you have a circumstance in your life, please don't worry.

~ Take it to *God* in prayer. ~

{Sh-h-h-h-h-h! The children are praying.}

Dear God,

Mom said whenever I'm worried about anything I can always come to You. Well, I need your help.

I'm worried about "corona," and all of the grownups are too. I don't think they know what to do. Someone said it's a virus, but it's not the flu. The whole world is talking about it every day. Will it ever go away?

While everyone's trying to figure out what to do, I thought maybe one of us should come and talk to You. I also wanna know about this thing called a "break-through." It's something my parents say when they talk to You. There's even a song about it too.

I wanna know God, "Can You "break-through" this virus called "corona?" Ple-e-e-e-ase break through it today, 'cuz Mom says You can do anything but fail.

Ps. I know You're listening, for Mom said You don't sleep. But, if there's something we need to do, please let me know that too. In Jesus' Name, I pray. Amen!

04.14.21

Dear God,

There's a lot going on down here. They closed our school yesterday. We have to stay in the house now. ...'Can't go outside and play. How are You doing Lord Jesus? ...Are You okay?

I haven't been here very long, but I can tell something's really wrong. Is there something that we need to do? Will it help turn things around if we all obey You?

I have one more question. "If Your door is always open, then why did they close the church?"

09.02.21

Dear God,

Somebody said adults don't pray like they used to, so, You probably have some extra time for me to talk to You.

I learned a new Bible verse today. It says we should humble ourselves when we pray; that we should turn away from evil, and seek Your face. Then, You'll hear our prayer, and heal our land. Does that mean You're coming to visit us from heaven?

We really need Your help here, Lord Jesus, because things haven't changed much since yesterday. Please come visit us soon. In Jesus' Name, I pray. Amen.

09.01.21

"If my people, which are called by my name, will humble themselves, and pray, and seek my face, and turn from their wicked ways; the will I hear from heaven, and will heal their land" {2 Chronicles 7:14}.

Dear God,

There's one more thing we need to talk about. This time it's a person. The person I'm referring to is responsible for all the schools. He's called a Su-per-in-ten-dent. He's the one who closed every school, and the reason why have to stay home too.

He doesn't seem to understand that I have no one to help me with school work when I get confused. I'm doing the best I can, but math is not so easy; and I need help with reading too. Can you do a break-through for us, so I can go back to school? In Jesus' Name, I pray. Amen.

08.29.21

Dear God,

It's me again. This time I'm a worried about all the grown-ups, because they're havin' a fuss. It's something about wearing the mask at school, as it relates to us. I don't mind wearing it, just as long as I can go to school; 'cuz I can take it off when I get there. That's what the other students do. Is it okay with You?

Can You help the parents get along so no one else gets hurt? Last night, we saw two parents scuffling in the dirt.

There's one more thing I need to ask You Lord. Can You {please} keep "corona" out? That's what all the parents are so worried about. I don't know who keeps bringin' this virus back to school; but it seems like we're gonna need another one of those break-throughs. In Jesus' Name, I pray. Amen.

08.29.21

Dear God,

Mom said, "The Holy Bible is Your Book," and that we should read it every day. I read my Bible today, and it said we should "…always pray." Does that mean we should pray all day, and all night too? I really need an answer, because Mom says I need at least 8 hours of sleep to be healthy. But, I'd rather stay up late and talk to You. Then, I can sleep in the next day.

I also wanted to know, "Do You need a break from all this trouble on earth?" And, I was wondering, "Do you ever take a nap?"

                      09.01.21

"…men ought always to pray" {Luke 18:1}.

Dear Heavenly Father and Dearest Lord Jesus,

I want to know if the two of You will agree with me on something, because Mom always says, "if two or three {of us} are gathered together in Your Name to agree on a subject in prayer, You will answer it." So, can we agree on some things tomorrow, because I'm making a list of the things I want to get?

I love you God! Thank you, in advance, for everything. In Jesus' Name, I pray. Amen.

11.10.21

"Again I say unto you, that if two of you shall agree on earth as touching anything that they shall ask, it shall be done for them of my Father which is in heaven. For where two or three are gathered together in my Name, there am I in the midst of them" {Matthew 18:19-20}.

Dear God,

Thank you for helping me at school. Everything's so much better since I've been having conversations with You. For the first time in a long time I felt like me, the way I used to feel before we had COVID-19.

I sleep better when I go to bed, and when I lay down, sweet dreams fill my head.

Thank You, Dear Lord for this wonderful day! I hope tomorrow is just like it was today. I love You so much!!! In Jesus' Name, I pray. Amen.

Ps. …Can't wait 'til morning. Good night! ☺

09.01.21

He will keep you in perfect peace, if you keep your mind on Him. {Read Isaiah 26:3NKJV}.

Dear God,

Mom says that You are everywhere, all of the time, and that You know everything! And when You created the world, You said everything that You made "was very good." Does that mean only goodness come from You?

Well I just have one question, "Can You use all of Your goodness to get rid of the corona virus, 'cuz the doctors still need Your help?"

Mom says I have to go to bed now. "…In Jesus' Name I pray. Amen."

Ps. I forgot to ask, "If You only created good people, where did all the mean ones come from?"

09.23.21

"And God saw everything that he had made, and, behold, it was very good" {Genesis 1:31a}.

Dear Heavenly Father,

Thank you for keeping our family safe, healthy, and "corona-free." Now I understand why mom wants us to be healthy and strong. So I eat my fruit and vegetables every day. I even exercise, before I go out to play.

And if the virus doesn't go away, help us to still be grateful every day.

In Jesus' Name, I pray. Amen.

Ps. I love You a so much, because You helped me grow strong during my "circumstance."

Pps. ...Hope it's almost over.

09.01.21

Dear God!

I pray for my principal, Mr. Peterboro, for my classmates, and all of my teachers at school. I pray for my friends, my family, and my neighbors too. Please bless my Mom and Dad, who I know love me. And help me be a better person--the best I can be. I want to help make the world a better place. I want change to begin within me. Heavenly Father, I love you with all of my heart! In Jesus' Name I pray. Amen. Good night.

11.20.21

Dear God!

I just wanted to say "Thank You" for today! It was a wonderful day. The weather was perfect; and I was able to go outside and play--without a mask. I feel so happy inside. ☺

Ps. Can we have another sunny day tomorrow please?

09.03.21

"A merry heart doeth good like a medicine" {Prov. 17:22}.

~ Choose Kindness ~

Whatever Happened to "Kindness?"

Whatever happened to kindness Mom?
Why did it go away?
Is it because of something I've said or done?
Or is it because of "corona" Mom?
How long is this virus gonna stay?

        05.11.21

A Cup of Kindness for You, and Me

I have enough kindness for you and me.
I want to change the world,
Though the future I cannot see.
I want to be one who makes a difference.
So I'm offering kindness,
Enough for you and me.

        05.13.21

I Promise Kindness

I promise I'll be kind to classmates at school,
I promise to obey my teachers,
...and to follow all the rules.
I'll show kindness to friends, and neighbors too,
For one day I may need kindness extended to me.
I know God will help me if I ask Him to.
As I am kind to others, just maybe,
Kindness will come back to me.

12.20.20

Pandemic Response --An Adult Perspective

This section was written for adults—young, old, and in-between, for all of us have been affected daily by the same dreadful news. As we reflect on the events of recent years, let us make room for laughter, and find something to smile about each day. Let us love one another, and forgive, so we can heal together.

Pandemic Response--An Adult Perspective

The first few poems in this section reflect life before the pandemic--from an adult perspective, and how our lives have changed since January, 2020; as we are yet, responding to it; adapting, and adjusting our lifestyles accordingly.

I call it *Pandemic Response—an Adult Perspective*, because we've been inundated with news flashes, breaking news, and daily briefings to keep us updated on the pandemic and the number of virus-related deaths since *"corona"* came. Coupled with all the other disappointing news, we must brace ourselves, and decide how to respond each day.

Life is a gift; and we are blessed to be alive after such a challenging period in our history. We have a reason to be joyful, and to celebrate life as we reflect on the pandemic in retrospect.

As we focus on staying healthy, let's give thanks, and show gratitude for the little blessings in life. Let's find meaningful ways to keep our mind constructively engaged, lend a helping hand to someone in need, and remember to laugh every day, for laughter is so good for the heart and soul.

"A merry heart doeth good like a medicine" {Prov. 17:22}.

A Reflection of Yesterday

Yesterday, I Was *Free!*

Yesterday I was *free!*
...Free to live and
Move about ease.

Freely, I could stand—anywhere.
And freely breathe in fresh air.
I was free to be me without a care.

Freely, I enjoyed the bluest skies,
Freely I could touch, laugh, or sigh.

Free to inhale or exhale deeply.
Living my happy life--joyfully.

Free to be me without glove or mask;
Free of hand sanitan* or quarantine-fuss.
It's {my} yesterday that I miss so much!

Freely I lived, I moved, and had my being.
. . .Freely I could touch all things.
With hope, I reflect on yesterday.

While I'm thankful and grateful to be alive,
I am hoping for yesterday's *freedoms*--again.

Mar., 2020

Hand sanitan -- hand sanitizer* ☺

"2020" -- In Retrospect

It's "2020"--the year a new decade began. But,
I like you, find myself at home--again.
Oh, I have plenty of gas and food to eat.
But, I like others, listen to news. I watch T.V.
It's something about a deadly virus
They call "Corona," COVID--19.

Don't quite know what to expect.
Don't really know what it means.
Things are quite different;
Not sure it'll ever be the same.
Oh, how much I miss the sweet life
I was livin' before "Corona" came.

04.08.21

Pandemic News:
"Is There Anything Else on T.V.?"

At First. . .

At first they called it "corona."
Now it's simply "COVID-19."
It doesn't matter what name they give it.
It's all the same to me.
Let's just say, "It's dangerous!"

05.11.21

Since "Corona" Came...

It's breaking news!
Something's happened!
But, they can't explain.

What is it?
A virus... A pandemic...
Does it have a name?

It's called "corona."
And it came from...
Sh-h-h-h-h! Don't say it!

...Can't say the country.
...Can't say the name.
...Can't talk about who's to blame.

But life as we knew it--is not the same.
'Cause everything's different since
"corona" came.

The whole world is different now,
Everything has changed. ...Don't think
It will ever be the same again.

05.11.21

Is There **Any Good News?**

Today is day number thirty-three.
...Still find myself at home, glued to T.V.
...Nothing on the channels but news
Updates--Federal, local, city, and state.
COVID deaths are increasing at alarming rates.

A cure is on the horizon they say.
Do you think we should. . . ?
Why can't we all just. . . ?
"STOP and Pray? ? ? ! ! !"

                        04.08.21

Closed, *for Now...*

Schools— **closed**. Offices— **closed**.
Churches— **closed**.
Home from work, and home-schooling—**24/7**.

From work-to-church, and church-to-school, at-home
Everything's changed since corona came.
From Hollywood-to-Broadway,
From Broadway-to-Maine
Everything stopped when corona came.

Businesses— **closed**. Business—lost.
...Can't survive a total shutdown--forever.
Out of business now—Some gone **forever.**

The factory, malls, and recital halls,
Closed for a short time to a longer duration; but
The grocer, bank, and gas station all remain--open.
They are essential operations to maintain life.

The lines are longer at the hardware store. It seems
Everyone's fix'n things up a little more.
The battle between parents and schools,
On schools being closed, or open, continues...
While life, as we know it, has forever changed.
Don't think it'll ever be the same...

Until we are fully open--again.

06.01.21

What if...?

What if this circumstance remains?
What if things stay the same?
What if this challenge I must endure?
I need to hold on to someone stronger, more secure,
One who provides comfort,
Who can help me endure.

What if I don't get a good report?
What if things don't change for me?
Just what if there is no cure? ? ?

I'll hold on to someone stronger, someone more secure,
One who can provide comfort,
And help me endure.

12.20.20

~

Can You Adjust? ? ?

Can you adjust, . . .when the whole world stops?
. . .When they say stay away--from each other?

~ No work! No play! ~

Can you adjust to waiting outside in the rain at your favorite store? Masks on. Sanitize your hands. "Stand six feet apart please. Okay, ...come on in."

Please keep your distance.
Thanks for your patience!

Do you need my assistance?
We're short of help; but, you'll be next.

How may I help you?
Sorry we don't have it. We can order it for you.

Thank you for your patience!
See you next time.

Can you adjust to the new way of doing things?
You must! We have too! All of us. . .

Adjustment made!

07.15.21

Chaos! ! !

Phone ringin' off the hook. . .
Last time I looked
I had an unlisted phone number in the book.
Telemarketers--Again! ! !

Election mess. . .
Total stress. . .
Stuck-at-home. . .
At times alone.

When I don't have the answer,
When I don't know what to do,

O' Dear God!

…So glad I can call on You; and
I've no doubt,
You can bring me through.

~

The solution to world chaos:

God! The Problem Solver.
Put your trust in Him.

04.08.21

"You, Lord, give true peace to those who depend on you, because they trust you" {Isaiah 26:3EXB}.

"A Pandemic Response"

It's called a pandemic. What should we do?
Well, I'm gonna trust God!
Oh Dear Lord, I call on You.

It's dangerous! They say it's worse than the "flu."
Well-l-l-l, I'm just gonna trust God!
Dear Lord, I'm calling on You.

They've closed our workplace, and shut down school.
. . .Don't know what else we can do.
Help us Dear Lord, …we need to hear from You.

They say, "Wash your hands and sing a song two, and
Be careful of surfaces around you. . ."
Dear Lord what should we do?
I'm back on my knees again. I'm calling on You!

"Wear a mask, and put some gloves on too."
Precious Lord! Hold my hand.
Help me get through.

I pray for our family, friends, and neighbors too.
Dear Lord, I'm leaning on, I rely on, …I trust in You.
…So thankful to have You

~

And I'm convinced, if we put our faith and trust in You,
No matter what course in life we choose,
I know, without a doubt,
You'll see us through.

05.05.21

The **"Good News"** is...

God desires to hear from us each day.
He asks that we humble ourselves, and
Pray, and when we seek Him,
Turn from our wicked ways. Then,
He not only hears us when we pray, but,
Promises to heal our land.
God cares, and He answers prayer.
That's "good news!"

        04.08.21

"If my people, which are called by my name, shall humble themselves, and pray, and seek my face, and turn from their wicked ways; then I will hear from heaven, and will forgive their sin, and will heal their land" {2 Chronicles 7:14KJV}.

While the World is Quiet
{What Will You Do?}

The world is quiet now, so what will you do?
...Go back to bed, rest your head on the pillow,
And wait for tomorrow's news?

If they say stay home, perhaps you should chill.
And, while all in the world is quiet and still,
Pray for those who've taken ill.

"Dear Heavenly Father, I come to You because
I know You love, and care for us.
I know You're listening, and don't require much.
Time is all you need for us to stay in touch.

Thank you for always being there for us!
I pray for friends and loved ones who aren't well,
That You'll heal them Lord and make them strong,
In Your presence give a joyful song!

Jesus, my Rock, I cling to You.
Comfort and strength I draw from You.
I'll be still so You can speak to me.
I'm listening; for sometimes You speak quietly.
Until then, I'll rest in You.

03.31.20

Speak to Me

"Dear God,"
I don't understand.
Right now, I need You.
Please hold my hand.
We have unanswered questions.
We don't understand.

When I get home
I need to hear You
Speak to me Lord Jesus.
I don't know what to do.
Speak, and I'll do
Whatever You tell me to.

05.11.21

"Gratitude" and "Sorrow"

"To everything there is a season, and a time to every purpose under the heaven: A time to be born, and a time to die; ...A time to weep, and a time to laugh; a time to mourn, and a time to dance; ...a time to embrace, and a time to refrain from embracing; A time to get and a time to lose; a time to keep, and a time to cast away; a time to tear, and a time to mend; a time to keep silence, and a time to speak; A time to love, and a time to hate; a time of war, and a time of peace" {Ecclesiastes 3:1-2, 4, 5-8}.

"Dad Love"

To all the Dads out there homeschooling:
We see you! We've heard about you too.
We want you to know we appreciate you,
And thank you for all that you do.
We lift our hats to you for helping us with
English, math, and science too.
For we have never been so confused.
Dad, we owe our earnest thanks to you!
We got through this semester
Because of your sacrifice.
We know we couldn't have done it without you.
You are a great Dad!

We love you!

To all the "great dads" out there, "Thank you!"

11.22.21

Honorable Mention

If rewards could be issued for things accomplished
  both great and small,
Our "Mom" would make the top of the list.
She does it all.
We'd probably run out of awards and trophies, and
I'm sure some things we'd miss.
But we can start by saying

"Thanks Mom," ...for everything you do,
For keeping us neat and comfortable too.
For pressing through the stress and tension,
You certainly deserve an honorable mention, and
At least a vacation or two.

For the tasks you do each day, and the way
You encourage us with the things you say,
Though it may seem to go unmentioned;
We just want to say, "Thank you, Mom,
For all that you do! For there is
No one in the world quite like you."

11.22.21

Flowers are a great way to say thanks. ☺

No Visitors Please

Hospitals, busy,
Quiet it's not!
Families patiently waiting
Though it seems they forgot.
It was not our intention; the
Hospital visits, we had to abate.
As if away, we had to vacate.

Registered nurses became
Caring nurse aids.
Cause the "virus" continued
To keep us away.

Can't visit our seniors
Who need us the most.
Must talk on the phone
No matter how close.

Because of the virus,
Loved ones--alone.
When will it end?
Nobody knows.
It's spreading and growing.
Seems out of control.

~ Coronavirus Alert! ~

05.13.21

Thank YOU "Essential Workers!"
{Gratitude}

Doctors and nurses what a sacrifice made,
Away from loved ones and home you've stayed.
The maintenance crew what a burden they bare,
Seldom pausing for much-needed fresh air.

Attending physicians rush thru hospital halls;
Pulmonologists remain on continuous call;
The virus directing the footsteps of all.

Sergeants, lieutenants, and the chiefs of police;
Captains, commissioners, and fireman chiefs;
Emergency vehicles with paramedic relief,
Each have endured endless trauma and grief.

Funeral homes and directors overwhelmed,
Counselors and therapists in full demand; it's a
Time to help each other, …lend a helping hand.
A time to look out for seniors living alone.

Grocery store baggers, cashiers, and stock clerks;
Managers, with support staff, so faithful at work.
Hats off to essential workers for all that you do.
We'll be forever grateful to you. We say,

Thank "YOU!!!"

05.13.21

We Need Each Other

We must finish all of our projects
And those things we started
Before the virus came through.

Plumbers, electricians, and repairmen,
We'll always need you.
Construction and masonry work must go on too.

Bus, and cab drivers, and truckers too,
Cargo transporters over land and sea,
Without rail trains in transit
Where would we be?

Pilots, co-pilots, and attendants-in-flight,
Air traffic controllers and mechanics
Working well into night.

Farmers, seed planters, and those in the field,
Auto workers in plants, where auto parts yield to
Software technicians in silence still;
All are essential workers-at-will.

If you don't see your title, I'd be remiss. Please
Use the lines below to add yours to the list.

_____

_____

10.06.21

Grief —Sorrow, Unbelief

We didn't grieve because You went
so quickly, ...without us being there.
It's so hard to believe you're no longer here.

Thought you'd be here long enough for us
to see you once more, and for us to say,
"I love you" again.
Though time passed quickly, it's hard
To close this {painful} door.
For grief and sadness remain.

Oh how we miss you _____!
...Still can't believe you're gone.

...Didn't have a chance to say good bye
the way we're accustomed to.
We think of you often. We loved you dearly.
We miss you so much!

Rest peacefully now...
We'll see you again on the other side.
Good-bye, Love.
And, please know--I'll always love you.
Rest peacefully. Good-bye for now.

05.13.21

Let "Us" Remember

Let "us" remember those we loved so dearly.
Let "us" remember their smile, and the laughter.
Let "us" remember forever and hereafter, and how
They helped "us" become who we are today.

Husband, wife, son and daughter,
Father, mother, sister and brother,
Grandpa and grandmother too;
Nephew, niece, aunt, and uncle;
Friend, we'll always remember you.

Family gatherings won't be the same without you;
So many joys and cares we shared too.
Forever, hereafter, we will always remember you.

With love, _____

05.11.21

As It Relates to Communication:
It's a Different World Now

Speak Freely, *If You Dare*!

Freedom of speech today, is rare.
So speak freely, if you dare!

On a note of caution, you might
Hold your thoughts to avoid the fuss.
Politically speaking, certain speech
can be dangerous.

You can't really say what you think,
Or express how you feel when
It comes to politics. For there are
Some friendships in need of mending,
And some may never heal.
~
Somewhere in that pile of rubbish
Are my thoughts from yesterday.
I had to do away with all of them, and pray;
For opinions are no longer received
as innocent thoughts.

05.20.21

Keep It to Yourself

Are you for, or against?
What does it matter?
I heard someone say through
All the chatter.

Last time she spoke up
She got a tap on the wrist.
That's because freedom of speech
No longer exists.

You may find it better not to say,
For those who were once with you
Now go the other way.

It's just better to keep your thoughts,
opinions, and good intentions to yourself.

08.12.21

A Matter of *Opinion*

Q. May I get your opinion? Do you have one?

A. I'd rather not say. It isn't good to have
   one {of those} these days.

~

Q. What do you think? Your opinion please. . .

A. I'm not going to tell you what I think or
   Which side I'm on, for I've learned from
   Previous conversations, not to have one.

~

Q. What's your opinion on the subject?

A. Well, . . .in my opinion, sometimes
   It's just better to be quiet. It's safer because
   If you keep your opinions to yourself,
   You won't lose your family and friends. ☺

~

My Opinion, or Yours?

My opinion (in response}: Does my opinion matter? Sure, it does! But no one really seems to care what we think anymore. It's nothing personal.

Your Opinion: Everyone is entitled to have their own opinion. Just use caution in how you express yourself, and with whom you choose to make it known.

08.12.21

When It Comes to Race, Creed or Color. . .
   . . .for the sake of humanity, let's just love one another!!!

2020 was a very tough year in other ways too, as physical, mental, and verbal abuse were often used. While physical and verbal abuse can lead to mental anguish, damaging words pierce the soul; and its' negative effects can last for a great duration.

While just one negative word can change the course of our lives, when it comes to race or color, rudeness--for no apparent reason--hurts, and can make you angry or sad.

If you have been abused, mistreated, or persecuted for any reason, it's not your fault that others choose to hate. The cure-all hatred is forgiveness. Are you willing to forgive?

What'd You Say? ? ?

Words hurt.
So, "be careful what you say!"

For the *"words"* you spoke yesterday,
Still hurt today!

Though you said, "I'm sorry"
. . .Couldn't pick myself up this time,
I wasn't able to clear my mind.

It's a little too late…
The *damage* is done.

Next time use caution before you speak,
For yesterday's *"words"* still hurt today.
~

May all *"your words,"* from now on be sweet,
As you carefully choose the words you speak.

Loving me first, means I can love you!
> *-- Half the battle is getting over the negative words that others have said about us. The other half is cancelling the negative words we've spoken over ourselves.*

04.05.21

Don't Hate!

Don't laugh at me 'cause I'm different!
Don't tease me 'cause I'm fat!
Don't shun me 'cause I'm brown-skinned.
Don't hate me because I'm white or black!
Let's try to get along.

Don't you know I didn't choose my color?
It came genetically through my father and mother,
…Pre-determined before my birth.
Let's try to live peaceably with one another
On this, our planet—earth.

Let's choose not to criticize.
Let's choose to love, instead of hate.
And those things we cannot change,
Accept them with love and grace.
Together, let us right the wrongs,
So we can get along today.

For every one of us--is darker, lighter,
Smaller, taller, bigger, brighter--different.
No two of us are {just} alike.
So let us appreciate one another,
And get along, and
Choose to love, instead of hate!

"…let us love one another; for love is of God"
{1 John4:7KJV}.

Beautiful in My Own **Skin**

Light skin, dark skin, or in-between,
The color of my skin doesn't define me.
With God as artist and creator.
We are a work of art–like tapestry;
All of us, together—His family.
Though the outer layer is what you see,
The real person I am, is my inner me.

Intricate in detail, we're more than just a name.
How boring it would be if we all looked the same.
We can honor God in our livin,' in showing
Kindness and respect for our fellow man,
We can use the gifts we've been given,
To improve and enhance the land.

As a part of His beautiful creation,
How much more beautiful we'd all be if
Each one of us in our own skin, race, ethnicity,
Demonstrated love unconditionally.
~
"We are beautiful—you and me!"

"Special Needs"- *a category placement given to one who has physical, emotional, behavioral, or learning challenges.*

"*Special* Needs," I'm *Not!*

God made me with tender hands.
He makes no mistakes.
Please understand when
He made me so unique,
He also had a plan.
But, *special needs*, I am not!

I'm "just me!"
And I welcome kindness from you. ☺

~

When you see someone who's different
Be kind!
For we are each uniquely different
in so many ways.

For I know *"I can do all things through Christ who strengthens me"* {Philippians 4:13}.

Healing is a Process

We live in a fallen world of imperfect people. We, ourselves, are imperfect. Though we desire to be loved and appreciated, sometimes we get hurt, and sometimes we hurt others. The sooner we forgive those who hurt us, the sooner we are able to heal; and the less harm we bring to ourselves. I call it "instant forgiveness," when we let go of all hurt, pain or disappointment the moment it happens. "Instant forgiveness" keeps us well, and is the key to enjoying optimum physical, emotional, and spiritual health. We enjoy wellness of mind, body, and spirit, when we free ourselves of past hurts, spiritual wounds, injury and disease. Many times we heal instantly, but sometimes healing is a process. Free yourself! Forgive! ...and allow your "self" to heal.

"Forgive, and ye shall be forgiven" (Luke 6: 37b).

Change the **Way** You Think

Posture poor
Feelin' low
Head down
No where to go.
Feelin' bad all by yo'self,
'Cause you're waddling in self-pity.
~
Head up to the sky
Shoulders back
Positively thinking
Little lack.

Opportunities comin' left and right
'Cause you're expectin' it in spite of the
"circumstance."

Life is better than it was,
All because I choose to live above the
"circumstance."

Now I see a brand new me.
No longer am I the person I used to be.
And I like it!

08.12.21

On the Positive...

I won't listen to negative conversation!
My schedule I can rearrange.
I promise not to worry about anything
I cannot do, or change.

~

Mending, and *Movin' On*...

I can change my situation if
I make up my mind to do it.

So, I'm *movin' on*... today.

I'm letting my feelings *mend* and *heal*.
Oh, what a difference it makes
When I pray!

04.15.21

"Heal me, Oh Lord, and I shall be healed; save me, and I shall be saved: for thou art my praise" (Jeremiah 17:14).

"Healing" – *at times we may need physical, financial, or emotional healing. Sometimes we need all three.*

I Will Heal
{"emotional" healing}

I'll do my best to follow a plan
In all of the affairs of life.
I'll try not to let things get behind.
I'll balance my books, and clear my mind.

I'll exercise, bathe, …maintain my health.
…brush my teeth, rinse well, and floss, and
Try to heal from sudden loss of activity;
…from holiday dinners we didn't have, and
…not connecting with family.

I'll heal from not seeing loved ones yesterday,
Both loved ones near, and far away.
And for the loved ones who've now passed away,
. . .*I will heal*—eventually.
I'm working on it today.

04.05.21

∼

"Weeping may endure for a night, but joy cometh in the morning" {Psalm 30:5bKJV}.

Prayer for "Restoration and Healing"

We forgive those who misled us
Concerning all things great and small.
We forgive those who lied and
Persecuted us long ago.
Yes, Lord, we forgive them all.

As You guide us, show us Your way.
Fill us with Your love today.

And for those times when we didn't
Know what to do,
Please forgive us Lord, for not {first}
Acknowledging You.

Cleanse and refresh us,
And our hearts—renew, as
You lead and guide us into all truth.

05.14.21

"Trust in the Lord with all your heart, and lean not unto your own understanding" {Proverbs 3:5}.

"Physical Healing" - *begins with faith, not doubt.*

Stand, *and* Believe

I'm standing on God's Word for healing
Until I see the victory.
I believe I'm healed of all infirmity,
For Jesus took those stripes for me,
Before He died on the cross at Calvary.

And this challenge, I believe I'll overcome.
I choose to believe I've already won.
Yes, I choose to believe it's already done.

And for the things in my body that still aren't right,
I'll walk by faith, and not by sight.
For I choose to believe
Change will come.

12.20.20

"Only believe" {Luke 8:50}.
"...by His stripes I am healed" {Isaiah 53:5}.

A Real Friend

Real friends, true friends, are hard to find. Choose your friends wisely.

"...there is a friend that sticketh closer than a brother"
{Proverbs 18:24b}.

Dear Heavenly Father,

Thank You for my health, my family, and for life itself. There's so much going on in the world, and I've been trying to live my life without You. I want to change that today. Today, I bring all of my cares, and concerns to You. Please forgive me of my sins—both known and unknown, for the way I've been living isn't Your best for me. Come into my heart Lord Jesus, and make it new, for I don't want to live another day without You. Thank You for giving Your life for me, and for dying on the cross at Calvary. I believe You were buried, and arose from the grave, and are now seated at the right hand of our Father, God. I accept Your promise of abundant life, and victory. Thank you for saving me now, for right now I am born again, in Jesus' Name, Amen.

_____

Your name

"If we confess our sins, he is faithful and just to forgive us our sins, and to cleanse us from all unrighteousness" {1 John 1:9}.

Today is Here

Today is here.
I've been hoping things would get better
I've been waiting for a change.

Even if it doesn't happen today,
I'll choose to be content.

And I won't worry about tomorrow,
...because life is much better now that
I have You.

03.31.21

"Trust in the Lord with all thine heart; and lean not unto thine own understanding" {Proverbs 3:5KJV}.

My Friend, Jesus

My Friend is always there for me;
He always has been, …always will be.
My thoughts I share with Him each day, for
He knows. He cares. He understands.
He has endless mercy, …He's full of grace.
I've learning to trust Him daily, by faith.

He's available right now—today;
Just like He was on yesterday.
When I don't sense His presence,
It's because …I stepped away.

I love spending time with Him,
He supplies my every need.
He would never leave, nor forsake me.
Jesus, You're my best friend;
A real friend You are indeed.

~

I no longer worry 'bout what others do or say,
What they think, or where they go.
I know God is with me always, and that
He loves me *so-o-o-o* much
More than I will ever know.

05.13.21

"Cast all your cares upon Him, for He careth for you"
{1 Peter 5:7}.

"Welcome J-o-y!"

Joy!

I'm thankful for His endless joy,
For it has been my strength.
Now when others see me,
They know who I've been with.

I smile. I sing. I'm happy.
In a way some don't seem to understand.
This is what it feels like when
Jesus holds your hand.

I'm livin' my best life with Jesus,
For in Him there's no regret.
In His presence is fullness of joy. . .
He hasn't failed me yet.

Are you looking for exuberant joy? ? ?
I found it in Jesus! ! !

07.04.21

"...in thy presence is fullness of joy..." {Psalm 16:11}.

The "Gift" of *Life*

I'm gonna live life;
I'm gonna laugh and play, and
Enjoy my life to the fullest every day.
I'll find my happy.
I won't complain,
For life is a "gift" from God!

Let "Joy" Inside

Be strong!
Stand tall!
Let joy inside!
As you take each breath,
Choose to live on the
Happy side of life!

12.20.20

"The joy of the Lord is my strength"
{Nehemiah 8:10}.

"…and Please Be Kind"

~ "Kindness" Pledge for daily living ~

I will:

Keep "love" in my heart.

Invest, and spend quality time with the Greatest Love of all.

Notice when others have a need, and lend a helping hand.

Do unto others what I'd want to have them do for me.

Notice, and appreciate, the good in others.

Encourage and lift up others.

Show that I care about the little things too.

Say kind words, beginning with my sister and brother.

Let *"kindness"* begin with me.

05.11.21

Little Life Lessons to "Live" by:

"Don't Wait"

Don't wait until you get bad news to start enjoying life. Decide now, to enjoy every moment of your day.

Don't wait until you are fatally ill to decide you'd rather be healthy. Practice good nutrition naturally. Enjoy good health today.

Don't wait until you lose your job to decide you'd rather be self-employed. Prepare in advance. Develop your innate gifts or talents so new doors can open.

Don't wait for your children to put into action everything you've been pouring into them. Be the best example every day of everything you want them to be, and believe they'll catch on, and mimic you.

Don't wait for your neighbor to be kind to you, because it may not happen. Extend kindness to your neighbor, because you may need him first.

Don't wait. Let your children know that life isn't always easy, that challenges will come. And as they experience each challenge, gently guide them through the many lessons of life.

Don't wait for adversity to happen before you embrace the beauty around you, because life will certainly pass you by. Take time to smell the roses, to see the sunset, and sunrise of each new day.

Don't wait for love to find you. Love your family, friends, and your neighbor, as you love yourself. Be a force-of-love in action, for love brings healing thru forgiveness; and love never fails.

05.13.21

Take Time! ...Do it Now

Take time to enjoy a walk in the park, and
Take time to inhale the beauty of creation.
Observe the beauty of each petal and leaf,
Have an appreciation for life's simplicities.

Take time to laugh, to smile, to sigh, to listen.
Pay attention to those who pass you by;
Enjoy the warmth that sunshine brings;
Appreciate the wind and rain that usher in
 the flowers of spring.

Take time to give thanks for the birds and the bees,
The green of the grass and tallest of trees.
Be ever grateful for each step you take,
As you give thanks to God for all He's made.

03.31.21

"In everything give thanks..." {1 Thessalonians 5:18}.

"Live"

Live in the moment.
Be present in each day.
For each second passes quickly.

Live with meaning.
Understand your purpose.
Always have good intentions.

Make an effort.
Strive to be your best.
For you only have one time to
Make a good impression, the **first** time.

03.31.21

Choose to "Live" Your Best Life Now!

Define greatness by the way you live.
Be the best!
...Give it your all!

Don't let others define who you are.
Be outstanding in, and through each test!
...Stand tall!

Live life to the fullest.
...Pursue happiness!
Live without regret

Life is a gift.
Choose to live it
The way it was meant to be.

      ----- Fill in the dash! ----
             12.30.21

As individuals we choose how we live life. We even get to choose our path. Each step we take along the way helps us fill in dash. Consider the narrow road.

"Enter through the narrow gate. For wide is the gate and broad is the road that leads to destruction, and many enter through it" {Matthew 7:13}.

"Live" Life--Give it Your All!

Define greatness by the way you live.
…Give it your all!
Be the best!

Be the best image of who you are,
With confident assurance,
…Stand tall!

Live your life with zest and zeal, and
One by one your achievements will
Lead to happiness.

You've been given the gift of life each day.
Keep living life the way it was meant to be.
With no regrets!

----- Fill in the dash! -----

11.04.21

There will be fewer distractions on the narrow road. Remember, it matters how we fill in the dash.

"But small is the gate and narrow the road that leads to life, and only a few find it" {Matthew 7:14}.

And remember to "just be" you!

Just Be **You!**
{Another *Little Life Lesson*}

Be the smarter one
Be the better one
Be an original
Be you!

Be the dependable one
Be there early, for to
Be early is to
Be on time!

Be available sometimes
Be there for someone else
Be genuine
Be real!

Be, because you can
Be, because you are
Be, because you desire to be...
Just be the best YOU, you can be! ! !

~

"Just Be You" was created for, and presented in the keynote address to scholarship recipients of the June, 2017 graduating class by Patrice Lee

I Wanna' Live Like Yesterday, ...Tomorrow

I wanna' live like I lived yesterday
...tomorrow, if that's okay
I wanna think the way I thought yesterday
...easy breezy and worry-free!

I wanna talk like I did yesterday--without a mask!
I only had to say it once
...didn't have to repeat as much.

I wanna shop like I did yesterday,
...didn't hoard anything.
And I had more than enough.

I wanna greet you like I did yesterday,
...without fear, if that's okay.

And tomorrow, when I see you,
I wanna give you a great big ol' hug.

03.31.21

~ A reflection ~

Only "Good" News!

I'm wearing my beautiful bright colors.
Hey, I've got on my favorite shoes.
And, when I get to my destination,
I'm only bringing good news.

I'm livin' like there's no tomorrow.
I'm celebrating each new day.
I'm gonna live, love, laugh, and play,
Like it was yesterday.
These happy feelings I just can't hide.
'Cause it feels so good to be alive!

02.03.22

"This is the day which the Lord hath made; we will rejoice and be glad in it" {Psalm 118:24}.

*May the God who created both heaven and earth,
keep you in perfect peace, as you keep
your mind stayed on Him.*

Want more Leep4Joy Books?

Leep4Joy Books are available at Barnesnoble.com, Barnes Noble stores, and on Amazon. We hope this collection of poems was a blessing to you, and welcome feedback from you. Write us at: Leep4Joy7@hotmail.com

Current List of Books

For Children:

Happy To Be Me!
The Bully Met My Dad! …and Became My Friend
Let's Love One Another
It's Just a CIRCUMSTANCE!
I Like Who I Am, I Love Being Me
It's About the BOYS!
Fit-not-Fat!
I've Got a CIRCUMSTANCE! …But I'm Gonna Be
   Just Fine {new release}

For Parents:

Mom, Dad, …Can We Talk? ? ?
Daddy! …Can You Hear Me? ? ?
Mommy, …Can You Hear Me? ? ?
Tips & Tools for a Safe and Healthy School Year

Best sellers: {en espanol}*

How to Overcome Every Obstacle and Land on Top *
Bully Me? …Oh No! ! ! {for Teens}
Bully me? …No More! ! ! *
Don't Be a Victim, Be Bully-Free

Made in the USA
Monee, IL
22 February 2022

91587412R00066